Sky gone

poems by

Sheryl White

Finishing Line Press
Georgetown, Kentucky

Sky gone

Copyright © 2020 by Sheryl White
ISBN 978-1-64662-296-2 First Edition
All rights reserved under International and Pan-American Copyright Conventions. No part of this book may be reproduced in any manner whatsoever without written permission from the publisher, except in the case of brief quotations embodied in critical articles and reviews.

ACKNOWLEDGMENTS

Thanks to the editor of *The Comstock Review* where Sky gone XI and Sky gone XV first appeared (under different titles).

I would like to extend thanks to Joyce for the two words, Stoneheart for encouraging words, Mark for so many supporting words, and my mother for the first word.

Publisher: Leah Huete de Maines
Editor: Christen Kincaid
Cover Art: Andrea J. Peters, *A Custard Sky II*, andreapetersart.com
Author Photo: Regina Mission
Cover Design: Elizabeth Maines McCleavy

Order online: www.finishinglinepress.com

Author inquiries and mail orders:
Finishing Line Press
P. O. Box 1626
Georgetown, Kentucky 40324
U. S. A.

Table of Contents

Sky gone I, January 1

Sky gone II 2

Sky gone III, February 3

Sky gone IV, March 4

Sky gone V, April 5

Sky gone VI, May 6

Sky gone VII, June 7

Sky gone VIII 8

Sky gone IX 9

Sky gone X, July 10

Sky gone XI 11

Sky gone XII 12

Sky gone XIII, August 13

Sky gone XIV 14

Sky gone XV, September 15

Sky gone XVI, October 16

Sky gone XVII, November 17

Sky XVIII 18

Sky gone XIX 19

Sky gone XX, December 20

Christmas Sky XXI 21

Morning Sky XXII 22

This Year's Sky XXIII 23

*Sky gone is in memory of my father,
Robert Buell White*

Sky gone I
> *January*

Sky gone, still from my window,
where there is no window, no light
absence, no heart larger, walls of flesh
and vein still beat, but breath gone, going
far up the sky. Gone shutters into night
endless, pulse, three hundred sixty-five
and counting down. We did not stop—
held his wrist tighter—did not demand
a recount, scene flash, the projection sliced
like slides vast on the whitest of screens.
Clouds covered the air's emptiness, wide
like what once was the sky, remember,
remember it was blue like our eyes.

Sky gone II

Dissolved as if it wasn't mine, forever
a cave too deep for rock-embalmed gems,
arches empty and wide, it waits on triumph,
parade, ranks of wonder, the white moment
a wave breaks, breaks the sand, the damp edge
of earth. In this time, time falters, eye first, the lens
that marks each shade. Fingers stretch or coil, a clutch
wasted, blue tints re-form into blue light, heart
particles float each valve, each vein, small griefs
to blood my world, inside out, my feet set over
nothing, unshod, there will be no more cold.

Sky gone III
> *February*

First
into year, into twenty-four
hours of never, numbers in sheets,
ice storms of transient glaze
hydrogen fed, cold stopped, sixty
minutes in the air of sixty. In the air
breath explodes, fired seconds change
hues to azure, its complement dreaded,
its heat the sum of the definition.

Then
far into heart, red,
dusted bones, branch free
elms, short, sterile, yearning.
Out here, one Jay, screech high
between rise and sun, wins home,
winded, limb tight. I hang on,
recumbent, not without dreams,
waked, not without memory.

Sky gone IV
    March

Under the rug, swept up and out
of sight, mind, the world known by us
as we know it, the day neither night
star-held, or day, night answered,
cloud-betrayed, no view uninterrupted
or reason to attend the seditious phases
of the moon. We have gravity so remain,
yet there is no fear of flying away,
nothing left above to scoop us up, tempt
us, short of breath, into the unknown.

Sky gone V
> *April*

Put away, closed, buttoned up
in its drab cloth coat, sealed and tied
with string, packed off, sent packing,
left on a doorstep, abandoned by
the side of the road. Who snapped
the closure, zipped, hooked and eyed
once the dust settled? The empty room
is just the empty room windowed on
nothing, nothing left in the house.

Sky gone VI
 May

Closeted for fear of censure, retribution
by the smog-gamed heavens, devalued, taken
for granted given, a constant buoyed
by any weather, any melt, any rain down
in the coal-driven bowel, beyond the rust-belted
plain of words. I cannot hold promise, I cannot
hold deliverance, its safety net, strung by new fliers
and eaters, sappers and their webs. Excretion scatters
high on limbed-up hemlocks, shelters higher
than poison can conquer, lower than effervescence
spewed, thawed, coughed up in the phlegm-
threaded rivers of lead and arsenic. Sludge
divulged by moments, hardens on an oil-
slicked albatross, feathers now a bower dark,
unhinged and hung in our secret place.

Sky gone VII
    June

From here, replaced by proxy, dark stuff,
litter of ash, broken buds, empty samaras
piled in the corner of a cloud, a cloud lost
like something half-dead at sea, float wood,
water soaked, lifting, sinking, brushed by the fin
of a dark thing, thrown up into a hole
without access or egress, sun barren. Infinite
mornings of fire—close, far, indeterminate
of distance—start just there in their hour, just
here in a meadow, clover bereft, bordered
by a forest of char, of nothing but
the forgotten fruit it grew from.

Sky gone VIII

January so long this year,
burials delayed, caskets piled
in funeral homes waiting for heat,
any change in light to thaw the ground,
turn the cold, relinquish the end
of my story. I kept his ring into August,
worked it hurt and rough with my spit
off my finger, its swell just too great
for an easy twist, an easy gone.

Sky gone IX
> *"Stooping in rhythm for whatever it was they might find."*
> —Colum McCann, TransAtlantic

It pretends a painful cerulean while my mother
sleeps, the only place she isn't gone, down, placed
under dreams and my father's cold short-cold
blanket. I have no words for her, no replacement
for the gone of anything. My own hovers level
with the horizon, waits for something else
to appear where the wide bruised arc blooms
empty, where color smears a shattered bowl, glaze
unfired blue, temporary, easy to chip and craze, color
that tears off in longing, in winding sheets. Easy
to imagine any other color. Not as easy to find
where color sleeps or how to wake it.

Sky gone X
> *July*

Closed for the season, see you
in my dreams, arrivederci baby.
Tomorrow and tomorrow and
was it something we said, or
didn't say, a stone left unturned,
an envelope unsealed? Did we leave
the baby in the bathwater? Hot
times ignored in the old town?
Today, windows lower, curbs gather
leaves, burnt and crumbling,
the side of the road sweeps
its tar into roots—bittersweet,
tree of heaven. Loosestrife, knotweed
slime the berms between forest,
highway. And the bugs eat their way
through hemlock, elm, ash, potluck,
BYO unnecessary. Each tree
takes a little piece of the wind
to heart, shield and callous makes
even in the absence of sky. Grief wields
a mighty sword, its cut, it's dry,
the spruce button up in green
overcoats, the chestnut looks for love
in all the wrong places.

Sky gone XI

In the black, the sickle moon, blue
weaned to the other side of my earth, right
sideup sidedown side, each camel
falls hump first, legs akimbo, all water drains,
spatters a starless field, a dark cloud-
colored wind knits its first scarf, tight rows
cast of thin new needles. Skeins to pearls
drop their cape over absence, a naked
abscess births above us. Someone retrieve
the cape, someone else find our night vision
glasses, our one-size-fits-all head gear.
Someone find the sky.

Sky gone XII

Black in its void, new penny
moon, gold fool, red stops
an old hush of bright ruined sand,
walls and fins burnished by
the tarted-up sun, cooled warm by
that gone sky. It pinches my eyes,
follows my own shadow, path-side,
shoulder-over, too proud
for day, too taut to spread its light
wing beyond up, down
eons of turreted muses, broken,
unmended, littered washes
dry with a rubble fertile until
hell freezes, the sun cracks, until
the sky returns.

Sky gone XIII
    August

The bird in the air sees white, no fly,
gnat. Nothing flying for the bat. Winged
things, things that glide, sail, soar,
hang far down on a cliff of soil, rot ferments
within each leaf that knew marvel, knows
only down, only closed death, overrated red
foils of fall. Green hovers at yellow, blue
absent. Blue a quick dream reflected in a slick
of river. Its other—its dark—drills into rock, earth,
waste—lightless, it floods loss over the bank.

Sky gone XIV

What point watching, eyes
stung open, quiet in their fierce
awake, face turned in its dark clothed
skin, light skin, stiff, thick, thin enough
to feel all the petals of the earth explode
in one silted blast—pink sprays of shattered
matter, enough to cover us complete, up
to our disbelief, to the point when our union
breaks broken, like when their wedding toss
rice appeared late, separate, hard grains
stuck between layers of yellowed silk?

Sky gone XV
September

First
to less, then a seed arcs, palms
its cup of sun between fingers, brilliant
in its void, red breaks into a thousand drifts,
while rudderless planets disrupt and canny whirl
with senseless direction. Follow true,
hold the line, pray out each knob on the rope.
Knots tighten, like clouds wefted of stiff cotton.
Somewhere in the middle row, Earth basks
in the join of a million cells, dead
these shot-starred years, these
holed overhead rips.

Again
while the wind decides,
wraps fog between mountain
foot and peak or keeps back fire
from saplings, half-formed chicks—
each understands only, if they stretch
too far, they stretch. Nothing about
the fall is known, if any wind does more
than stir, lift feathers, leaves, nothing
known if any sky is there at all, if
any sky is needed.

Sky gone XVI
October

So welcome gone, in its wake, fall-
full moon, snow silvered, star framed arch
of transit, just this side of kiss, this side
longed for melt, a moment delivered,
tight, hands as shawl, flesh warm
wrapped, worn with touch, under
November's low arc of black, under
cover of absence, fine white.

Sky gone XVII
> *November*

No matter, scarlet roars over the red
maple, side by ochre-leafed tulip poplars,
ginkgos, webs of gilt hues, taken in by the air,
thrust into heaven on strong, silver-laced limbs,
top lit, or down, bottom shadowed. Pines swing,
scaffolds of mirth, high above root anchor. How far,
or long, how fool to accept any replacement,
exchange? Overcome by this fatal breath of fall,
the open mouth of an empty sky inhales, color-
full, looks to get its own back.

Sky gone XVIII

*"You may do this, I tell you, it is permitted.
Begin again the story of your life." —Jane Hirshfield, Da Capo*

Again, below or too above, level
with my eye, askance, peripheral, dead
on center—none of this. A blue past, thunder
holder, rain midwife, it was something—
a big deal, super arc, hull of cloud, hanger
for the crow, the red tail, each bee drone,
angel and angel maker. Throw the earth wet
high, sow islands over my head, simple
canopies of earthen silk, whistle the moth,
the evolved beetle, net and tag starlings
with discrimination, tight bow bag, careful
the egg. Provide seed, ginkgo, pine—
white, red, black—raise a hedge, dig a moat.
Let us figure out how to get there, and
what to call the new ocean.

Sky gone XIX

So we packed our bags, heavy
with assumptions in the lining, answers
wrapped in an extra case, stained
at the seams. If we walked
a thousand miles, we walked
back and forth up the switchback
of the world, long days taken to cross
Atlantic pools, search small caves
along each shore. We brought copies
of *Goodnight Moon* for the children, damp,
we stockpiled peanut butter, cans
of tuna sealed in packs of three. More
days and a desert crossing, water
was gone, bayous, creeks overflowed
too far south, our collateral
misjudgment followed us in dying
white pine forests, we remembered
melt, grave solitary stones and
yards of bones. Animals we knew
from the ark or zoo? Once answered,
we were beckoned—pitch your tent,
unpack, lie down, imagine stars.

Sky XX
December

Not yet one year gone, light hues
break upon the earth, swish and the bird
is other, look up, stars, clouds
invent a face, reinvent form above oak
and pine, mimic true, unfurl their new-lit
banners. A flag sure, mast high, waves,
no hands left, still, bone has its memory,
skin shivers, a pulse, again wrist-held.
On your day, no cake, no gift. I will hold
my breath, dream of small fires mirrored
in my mother's eyes, fires to ash. Ash
sifts down through my fingers, down
to earth then up again into the sky.

Christmas Sky XXI

Sky as god, her strong-armed stretch
skin blue. Thin fingers of beech and birch
beckon in quiet reach, winter boles shed—
jagged tears, rough skins, straight
never. Wind inhabits space between angles,
settles steady in the old ribbed branches. Birthing
bark carries new buds. Between their hold, leaf,
fruit, *Corylus* catkin, hazel swells. While mute
below snow, something waits, not frozen,
not yet melt but paused ready. Roots creep, pull
loose earth taut, plant promise as answer
to the question we imagined—how
to rise, how to reach heaven.

Morning Sky XXII

This gray on blue, this light
on bark, gold scents the air, sweet
shadow, short in mourning, leaves—
left through this winter, hang, tremble—
gone lives tethered slim to thin red
limbs. I ache to step into this, move
one foot in front of the other, unbow
my head and walk out into the shortest
month, the stilled bird song, the
forgiving soil, dark marked shallow by
so many footprints leading away.

This Year's Sky XXIII

It is here in the garden, above and around
salvia celebrants, umbrella pine, bursts of 'Morning
Light' *Miscanthus*. After the night rain, dawn
strips into full, into glisten, marmalade
dahlias and the gifted gold of each last
daisy's eye. Appetites cease, beginnings lost
to the senescence of the leaf, but ends, awaited
ends, celebrated. Where there is no blue, color plays
like color burnished, a vein highlight over rouged
leaves, every glisten of seed head, fruit blush,
every berry, the perfect berry, fallen to earth
under the vast, waked sky.

This Year's Sky XXIII

It is here in the garden, above and around
salvia celebrants, umbrella pine, bursts of 'Morning
Light' *Miscanthus*. After the night rain, dawn
strips into full, into glisten, marmalade
dahlias and the gifted gold of each last
daisy's eye. Appetites cease, beginnings lost
to the senescence of the leaf, but ends, awaited
ends, celebrated. Where there is no blue, color plays
like color burnished, a vein highlight over rouged
leaves, every glisten of seed head, fruit blush,
every berry, the perfect berry, fallen to earth
under the vast, waked sky.

Sheryl White is an artist and writer living in Boston. Her writing has been published in *Ibbetson Street Press, Blast Furnace, Solstice Literary Magazine, Poetry Quarterly, The Boston Globe, Halfway Down the Stairs, Split Rock Review, Gravel, The Woven Tale Press Journal,* and *The Comstock Review*. In 2016, she received a Massachusetts Cultural Council Poetry Finalist Grant and was selected in 2016 and 2017 for the Mayor of Boston Poetry Program.

As a fine artist, with a BFA from the University of Michigan, she has a long list of exhibitions for her paintings—solo, group, invitational, juried—as well as being a MacDowell fellow. Her work is included in deCordova Museum's Corporate Art Loan Program in Lincoln, MA.

White works at the Arnold Arboretum of Harvard University as the Coordinator of Visitor Engagement and Exhibitions, where she has written for various in-house platforms and curates their art shows. As a board member of Roslindale Green & Clean, an advocacy and educational nonprofit, she is a frequent contributor of newsletter articles and other publicity and organizational publications.

White has an award-winning garden in Boston's Roslindale neighborhood where she lives with her husband. She has adult daughters in Chicago and in Montana, where there are also three wonderful grandsons and a son-in-law.

Sky gone is in memory of her father.

www.ingramcontent.com/pod-product-compliance
Lightning Source LLC
LaVergne TN
LVHW041520070426
835507LV00012B/1702